Suki and the Case of the Lost Bunnies

Written by Lucy Floyd

Illustrated by Kathleen Howell

I am Suki Wong. I find lost things.

And I find lost things for everybody.
I find things for families. I find things for
kids. I even find things for babies.

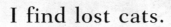
I find lost cats.

I find lost hats.

I find lost puppies.

I find lost guppies.

Once I had a very hard case. It was The Case of the Lost Bunnies. It began when I heard Sam crying.

Sam lives next door to me.

Sam's mom and dad work. So Mrs. Jones takes care of Sam.

I hurried next door when I heard Sam crying.

"Why is Sam crying?" I said.

"He says he wants his bunnies,"
Mrs. Jones said.

"My bunnies are lost!" Sam cried.

"Here is a bunny!" Mrs. Jones said. "Now your bunny is not lost."

"NO! Not my bunnies!" Sam cried. "My bunnies hop. My bunnies hop up and down!"

"I, Suki Wong, find lost things," I said. "I will look for the bunnies."

I tried to find the bunnies. I looked
under a table. I looked under a chair.
No bunnies!

I went to Sam's room. I looked under the bed. I emptied out the toy box. And I found two toy bunnies.

I carried the bunnies to Sam. "Look, Sam. Here are your bunnies," I said.

"NO! Not my bunnies!" Sam cried. "My bunnies hop. My bunnies hop up and down!"

"I, Suki Wong, find lost things," I said. "I will try to find the bunnies."

I hurried back to Sam's room. I looked in the closet. I emptied out a drawer. And I found a shirt with bunnies on it.

I carried the shirt to Sam. "Look, Sam. Here are your bunnies," I said.

"NO! Not my bunnies!" Sam cried. "My bunnies hop. My bunnies hop up and down!"

"I will keep trying to find the bunnies," I said.

Maybe Sam had books about bunnies. I found a box of books. I emptied out the box. And I found some stories about bunnies.

I carried the book to Sam. "Look, Sam. Here are your bunnies. See, all of these stories are about bunnies."

"NO! Not my bunnies!" Sam cried. "My bunnies hop. My bunnies hop up and down!"

I tried again to find the bunnies. I went to the kitchen. I saw a cup in the sink. The cup had bunnies on it. I emptied out the water and dried the cup.

I carried the cup to Sam. "Look, Sam. Here are your bunnies," I said.

"NO! Not my bunnies!" Sam cried. "My bunnies hop. My bunnies hop up and down!"

I, Suki Wong, find lost things. But where were the bunnies?

I hurried to the bathroom. I looked in the tub. I looked on the shelf. I looked at the towels drying on the rack. No bunnies!

I hurried to the room where clothes are washed and dried. I looked in the basket. I looked in the washer. No bunnies!

Then Sam came into the room. He ran to the dryer. "MY BUNNIES!" he cried.

"See!" said Sam. "My bunnies hop! My bunnies hop up and down!"

I, Suki Wong, find lost things. But sometimes I need a little help.